TRAMPOLINING for all ages

Contents

History of Trampolining

The origins of trampolining as an entertainment are lost in antiquity. Through the ages people have bounced up and down for pleasure, diversion and public enjoyment on a variety of springy devices. These devices included supple planks placed on blocks, springboards of all kinds used by "Leapers", skin stretched between stakes, safety nets and, of course, conventional beds. The word trampoline means springboard and is derived from the Spanish and German.

Trampolining as a sport and a branch of physical education really began when a young American Diving and Tumbling Champion called George Nissen cleared out his father's garage and began making the first trampoline designed for school and college use. Aided by the physical education experts he recruited for his staff, he produced text books, wall charts, lessons, schemes and training aids of all kinds.

The first trampoline authorised for use as part of an English school's physical education programme was installed in Loxford School, Ilford, in 1949. The apparatus was cumbersome and non-folding and learning was largely by trial and error. However, there were no accidents and progress was rapid.

It was soon realised that no special skill or physique was required to become quite proficient, and provided certain safety precautions were taken everybody, including handicapped pupils, got fun and real physical benefit from the widest range of movements ever made possible by one single piece of apparatus. From 1949 to 1956 progress in trampolining as a sport was slow but sure. Boys learned in a few weeks advanced tumbling tricks that previously had taken men years to master. Natural spring was developed bringing improvements in vaulting and agility and enthusiasm for physical activity.

In 1956 manufacture of reliable folding trampolines began and teachers' courses were organised. In 1959 the Amateur Gymnastic Association staged the first British National Trampoline Championships with nearly 60 entrants and Annual Trampoline Championships have taken place each year since then in almost every country in Europe. International Matches began in 1961 at Kiel with a competition between England and Germany. The First and Second World Trampoline Championships were held in London in 1964 & 1965, the Third in the U.S.A. in 1966, and London again in 1967.

The sport continues to grow rapidly. Trampolines are now standard equipment along with footballs, cricket gear, etc., in many of the nation's schools and Local and National Associations have been formed to further the growth of the sport.

What is Trampolining?

It is fun and exercise obtained from bouncing up and down, forward and backward, round and round on the centre of a tight but resilient nylon sheet stretched between a steel frame and supported by elastic or steel springs.

This enables you to jump higher than ever before, remain in the air longer giving more time to perform, extend and combine in difficulty all the conventional leaps, turns, twists and somersaults.

It also permits bouncing, rolling, twisting, landing and taking off with continuous rebounds from the feet, knees, seat, back, front, hands and knees. These actions only being limited by the performer's stamina and practice.

It is an activity for all ages and both sexes.

It gives physically handicapped people the chance to enjoy the power and exhilaration of jumping, falling and rebounding without injury.

It is an intensive conditioning exercise which makes strong demands on the circulation and respiration necessitating practice in short spells only.

It offers a range and complexity of movement combinations to challenge even the most endowed and accomplished gymnast.

It is an officially recognised physical education activity.

It is a competitive event and a sport in its own right.

It is a means of practising diving skills without the need to get wet or even be able to swim.

Finally it is easy to learn, straightforward to teach, difficult to master completely and almost hopeless to give up.

Learning Gradually

Most things worth learning take time. Becoming an expert trampolinist takes time—time spent in understanding and mastering each step before moving on to the next. Confidence should not be confused with recklessness; the former is built on knowledge, the latter on ignorance. Master all the fundamental bounces before trying somersaults and other advanced activities. Get to know and respect the apparatus through progressive stages.

It is a good idea to attend a course on trampoline work and try to analyse all the movements. It will then be found that even the most difficult exercises can be broken down into simple movements that can be practised and mastered separately. When the parts or easier movements are mastered, they can then be joined together gradually before moving to a more demanding exercise or combination of movements.

Equipment Types

The minimum and maximum sizes of trampolines allowed to be used at competitions are:

Height of frame   0.95—1.05 metres
Length of bed   3.60—4.30 metres
Width of bed   1.80—2.15 metres

Most people prefer the Goliath or larger models.

The best type of frame folds and unfolds in seconds and wheels away on a roller stand. Non-folding trampolines are not recommended as they are awkward, take up a lot of space and because they are difficult to put away there is a considerable risk of accidents through unsupervised use. Pit models consisting of metal frames fixed over and supported by the walls of the pit, have had some popularity but are only used in amusement parks.

Trampoline beds vary in performance, cost and wear, according to the material and construction. The cheapest are cotton, duck or linen sheet beds. The disadvantages of this type of bed are that it tends to stretch in length with use and also absorbs moisture which makes it heavier on damp days. It can also split without warning and is very rough surfaced and can easily injure the performer's skin.

Medium priced sheet nylon, double or single thickness, is good value and very suitable for ordinary school use. One disadvantage is that the bed acts as a giant sail and some of the energy expended by the performer is wasted in moving large masses of air above and below the bed.

Woven nylon webbing stitched under tension makes the best bed. The open woven construction allows air to pass through the bed and most of the energy expended by the performer is available for lift. The landings are also softer. These beds are more expensive but are usually chosen for competition work.

The "lift" of a bed comes from the extension recoil of the suspension system linking the bed with the frame. Two suspension systems are used: elastic shock cord cable or steel springs. Elastic cords clipped into circular cables or in double parallel strands are lighter in weight, although slightly slower in motion than steel springs. They are also softer to land on if the performer accidentally moves from the middle of the bed.

Steel springs, however, if fitted and used properly, can give many years of satisfactory use and are probably best for the larger Goliath beds.

For maximum protection, clip-on washable pads are used on the frame to protect the performer should he fall against the frame. All school Trampolines should have effective frame pads.

Precautions

Remember that at least two people are required for folding, unfolding or moving a trampoline.

Certain precautions must be taken **before you begin jumping** and after you have finished. They include the following:—

1. Before erecting the trampoline know exactly how to unfold it safely—at least two people are needed for safety.
2. Make sure all the leg braces of the trampoline are secured and all cables and spring hooks are pointing downwards.
3. Make sure you have at least 16ft. headroom from floor to lowest overhanging obstacle. This includes the belt in any overhead spotting rig.
4. Make sure that you have at least four (spotters) standing by, one on each side of the trampoline ready to assist you if you move towards the frame edge.
5. Remove your spectacles if loose and take all hard objects out of your pockets.
6. Wear flexible light footwear and clothing that allows a full range of movement.
7. Know where the first aid box is.
8. Know how to fold the trampoline properly when finished with and lock it up and padlock securely.

Safety Rules

The following rules apply **when you begin jumping:**

1. Always get permission from the instructor before attempting any new work. Know and work within your limitations.
2. Jump for short periods only, about 40 seconds is long enough. Never get on until the previous jumper is off.
3. Keep the height of jumping down until you have full control, about 15 ins. height is quite sufficient at first.
4. Keep all jumping in the middle of the bed. Remember, it is better to land in the middle of the bed from a somersault even if it is only on your back or on your seat rather than to land near the frame on your feet.
5. Always use overhead spotting rig safety belt when learning advanced movements, see page 37.
6. Never use the trampoline on your own, always have spotters standing ready.
7. Never play the fool on the trampoline bed.

Photo: M. Topp

ILLUSTRATIONS

In order to make the illustrations in this book clear, the figures have been drawn separated across the page. In fact most of the movements take place on and above the centre of the bed (as shown here) and the performer does not move horizontally. The photograph shows R. Walker, Regent Street Polytechnic Lecturer in Physical Education, performing the tucked back somersault.

Spotting

This word has three meanings: —

(a) When referring to a performer doing every bounce in the centre of the bed—the ultimate aim of the skilled trampolinist.

(b) Assistants helping or being ready to help a performer by standing at each side of the trampoline top rail, or by holding a performer in a belt or by jumping with him, or being on the side of the bed ready to move in and assist if required.

(c) Sighting the bed between multiple somersaults with twists, or back or front drop landings, in order to check if rotation or twist needs slowing or speeding up.

In a well-conducted class, spotting at the side rail is always apparent but should rarely be necessary.

There should always be four spotters in attendance, one along each end rail and one along each side rail. Their body weight is forward, hands on top of the pads on the rail ready to push if required. Their gaze is fixed all the time on the performer's waist, they assist merely by pushing the performer if and when he comes towards them. It is the performer's responsibility to see that the spotters are in place and that they know what he is going to do and when to expect him to do it.

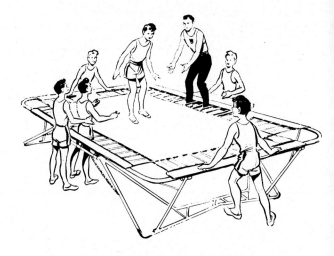

Normally the spotters would be standing on the ground but this sketch shows alternative positions.

On the left 2 strands have been removed and the spotter stands on the ground or he can stand on a box to get to the right height. The man on the right is shown standing between these strands on a table.

Fitting safety sides with extra tubing and wide frame pads to make a proper coaching platform all down each side, is the safest and most efficient provision.

Climbing On

A low box placed at the end of the trampoline will speed up getting on the apparatus.

Always step from the frame directly on to the bed. Later, after more experience has been gained, a forward roll on to the bed makes an attractive mount in keeping with the exercise. There must only be one jumper at a time on the bed.

Getting Off

Beginners should never jump directly from the bed to the frame or the ground because of the unexpected shock of the hard ground after the softness of the trampoline. The bouncing should first be checked, see page 10, and then a firm walk to the edge of the bed; place a hand on the frame and step down.

Various different dismounts can be learned later, see page 43, but beginners are well advised to step off until more experienced.

Vertical Foot Bouncing

Foot bouncing is the most important bounce in trampolining as it usually precedes every other bounce. If the foot bounce is poorly done all following work will almost certainly be badly performed. This should be the first exercise on the trampoline and it should be practised until perfect control is obtained.

All bouncing should be vertical, that is directly up and down. The following points, already listed, are repeated for emphasis:—

(a) The bouncing must always be done in the middle of the bed i.e., on the "spot".

(b) Start with the feet about hip width apart at take-off and also on landing. After a little practice the feet can be pulled together as the body rises and then opened out again for landing.

(c) The body should be erect but not stiff.

(d) The eyes should be fixed on the end of the bed or frame.

(e) The arms should circle forwards and upwards as the body rises, and sideways and downwards as the body falls. Never swing your arms behind your head because this will spoil your balance.

(f) Don't jump too high; about 15 in. is high enough.

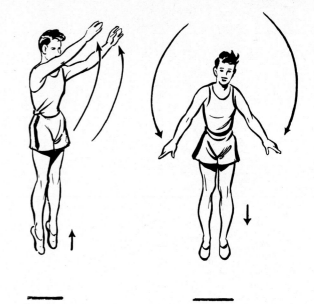

GOING UP

Arms forwards and upwards with vigorous push.

COMING DOWN

Arms out sideways and downwards, moving behind the body after passing the shoulder-line and changing to a strong upward swing to increase height.

VERTICAL FOOT BOUNCING—continued

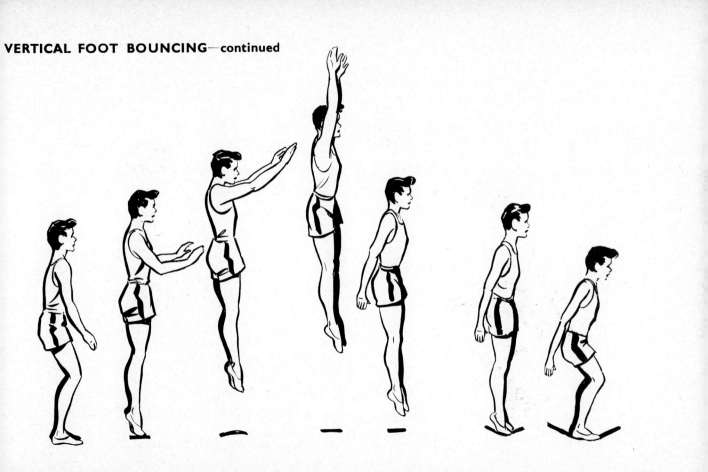

Checking the Bounce

To stop bouncing at the end of an exercise or in an emergency, place the feet flat on the bed and bend the knees and hips so that the legs absorb the recoil of the bed.

Place the arms forward at about 45° outwards in order to keep balanced. Adjoining sketch shows the check bounce position approximately.

Variations of the Foot Bounce

The three positions shown here are easy to learn, spectacular to watch, exciting to do and also very valuable control exercises for beginners and experts alike.

TUCK JUMPING

Keep trunk erect.

Take knees up to chest, don't bend chest down to your knees.

Place hands on shins as shown.

PIKED JUMPING

Keep trunk as erect as possible but it will move forward more than the tuck jump.

Point toes and touch upper insteps.

PIKED STRADDLE JUMPING

Similar to the Pike Jump, but with the legs out sideways as far as possible. This is a very spectacular exercise when done properly and looks nice in competition routines.

Landing Positions

Seat bouncing, knee bouncing, front drop and back drop, are complete exercises in themselves for beginners, but later they form links between sequences, beginnings or finishes for other exercises. They are therefore very important. These are the fundamentals of trampoline work and they must be perfected before moving on to other work. The front drop and back drop are also steps to turning forwards and backwards in a simple and safe way which will be useful when somersault movements are tackled later on.

The sketches on these two pages show the proper landing positions and if these are performed correctly, return to the starting position will be automatic.

It is recommended that each of these be taken from stationary positions, without preliminary foot bouncing and that they be checked to see they are correct. It is very important to land exactly in the manner shown.

Remember that there is no need to jump high to go into these landing positions. Try them at first from a standing position and then add height gradually as explained in the following pages.

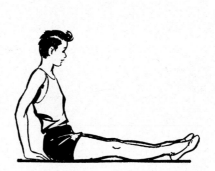

SEAT LANDING

Legs straight, calves on bed, trunk leaning slightly backwards.

Hands to the rear of seat, fingers pointing forwards to keep elbow joints flexible.

KNEE LANDING

Keep trunk erect but not stiff.

Never arch back.

Point toes backwards.

Practise bouncing around on knees first before dropping down on to knees from a standing position.

HANDS AND KNEES LANDING

This is a simple development from knee landing, body weight remaining back on knees.

Hands are only used as steadiers. This position makes a good lead into front drop.

FRONT DROP LANDING

Practise first from a hands and knees position by extending legs backwards.

Elbows out sideways, fingers pointing inwards towards body.

Hold head clear of the bed and allow abdomen to sink into the bed.

Do not break fall with hands, weight should be on abdomen and thighs.

BACK DROP LANDING

Head forward, arms forward and hips forward.

Tighten neck muscles by tucking in chin to prevent a whiplash of head when landing on back.

Remember to lift hips rather than legs so as to keep seat off the bed.

Failure is usually due to not keeping arms and hips forward in backward fall.

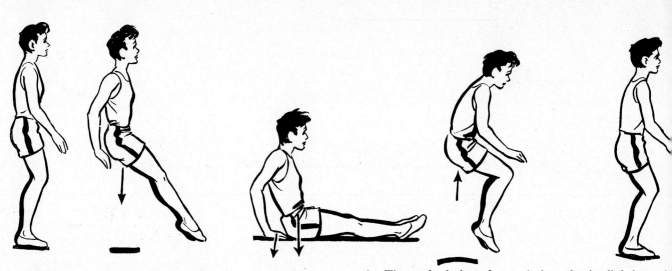

Feet to Seat Bouncing

This bounce can be done from a standing position on the bed.   There is no need to jump. Lean backwards and thrust feet forwards but not upwards and place hands in the rear of seat to make a landing as shown in the third sketch.

If the landing is made correctly, return to a standing position will be automatic.

1. Start from standing position, later on you can jump.

2. Thrust both legs forward, lean back slightly and sit down.

3. Legs straight, calves on bed, trunk slightly backwards, hands to rear of seat, fingers pointing forwards.

4. Because you leaned back as you sat down the trampoline will automatically pitch you forward on to feet if you bend knees slightly.

5. From this position go straight into another seat bounce, adding a little more lift as you become more skilful.

Feet to Knees Bouncing

Same starting position as on page 14. Try this bounce first by starting on the knees as shown in the middle figure.

When you feel confident, bounce up to feet. Then from standing, bounce down on to the knees then up to feet again. Later perform from a jump as shown above

Toes back. Trunk erect but not stiff. Knees apart
Swing arms upward to give lift.
Repeat this exercise 5 times.

Now try going from seat to knees and then knees to seat to combine these two exercises into a sequence

Feet to Hands-and-Knees Bouncing

Extend the knees then flex the knees and drop on to the knees, toes pointing backwards, trunk inclined slightly forwards. Hands should be touching the bed lightly at the same time as the knees but not taking much weight; they are simply to maintain balance.

Return bounce to feet.

Feet to Front Bouncing

Before starting from feet position practise starting from the hands and knees landing position. Extend legs backwards and drop flat on to the bed with hands palm downwards, elbows out. The important thing is to allow tummy to sink into the bed and not to break fall with hands.

Never dive forward—this is caused by leaning into the movement.

Next, practise starting from a semi-crouched standing position with the hands in a ready position, fingers pointing inwards and elbows out. Extend the legs gently and carry them straight backwards so that the tummy drops exactly where the feet were.

Never drop with the back arched. Keep the trunk flexed until nearly down, then open out with legs going back.

Recovery is almost automatic if the landing position is correct and a little push is given with the hands.

Repeat this exercise 5 times.

The next step is to try this front drop to hands and knees then front drop to seat bounce. To do this give a stronger push with your hands as you rise from the front drop, and lean well backwards to land in the feet drop position.

Feet to Back Bouncing

This is a little more difficult to do than the other bounces because it is unusual to fall backwards without looking backwards and without trying to protect oneself from falling.

First, try the position on the bed. Keep head well forward, neck muscles tensed with chin tucked well in. Arms should be well forward and hips up as far as possible, legs at about 45° to body with the knee joint loose.

Now stand on the bed with head forward, chin tucked in and neck muscles tight. Put arms well forward then thrust hips forward as far as possible and gently lift one knee, keeping the hips forward until you fall down on to your back. Arms should still be forward when landing. If the landing position is correct you will bounce back on to your feet immediately.

The pictures on page 19 now show you the sequence of events doing this bounce from the feet position.

1. 2. Lift hips in take-off, try to let waist fall where feet left the bed.

3. 4. Keep neck muscles tense to avoid whiplash of head. Note arms are still out in front.

5. 6. It is important to keep arms forward for a good landing. If you put them back you will fall back

Twisting

In trampoline language twisting means the ability to rotate on the vertical axis of head and feet. This is best done when your body is straight.

If body is bent during a bounce it should be straightened before a twist can be done. After the twist is completed, body can then be bent again.

To twist to the left, turn head and look in that direction after take-off and move the right shoulder or arm if a strong twist is needed in the direction you want to turn, that is over to the left.

To turn to the right, turn head to the right and look to the right, and bring left arm and shoulder across.

Remember, a twist must not be started until you have left the bed, otherwise you will fall towards the side of the trampoline.

This diagram shows that with the arms extended, the twist will be slow, and with the arms close to the body, the twist will be rapid.

To stop a twist, therefore, put arms out.

To speed up a twist after throwing your arms out to get it going, wrap up your arms as shown in the diagram.

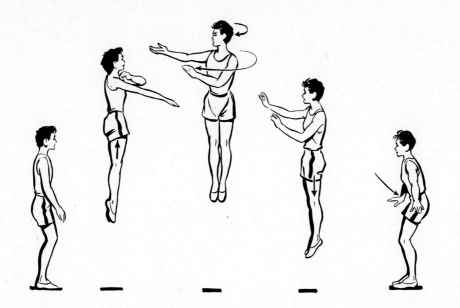

Feet Bounce and Twist to the Right

Practise vertical bouncing and twisting to left and right using the head and arm as explained. Start with a half twist and gradually build up to a full twist. Remember the important thing is not to start twisting until you have left the bed. Take care to keep height down and aim at control of the twist. Gradually you can build up to double twisting quite easily, adding height as you gain control.

Practise twisting to both sides and then you will discover which is your better way.

Swivel Hips

Once you have learnt how to twist on a vertical jump you can then put this on to one of the fundamental bounces. The first one to practise is the seat bounce with half twist known as the swivel hips.

First get a perfect seat bounce, because if this is not performed well it will be difficult to do a good swivel in between the seat bounces.

Break down the swivel hips into stages as follows:—

(a) Develop a good seat bounce with plenty of lift with arms stretching above head.

(b) As the arms swing upwards above the head, bring one arm across face to initiate the twist. Land on the feet facing in the opposite direction.

(c) Continue practising until you take the twist high enough and quickly enough to allow you to extend your feet and make a seat bounce landing after the twist has been made.

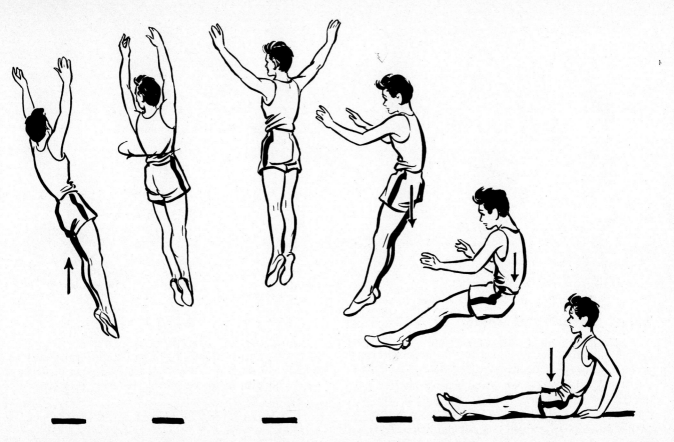

Front Drop Half Twist to Back

Before you can do this bounce well, you have to perfect the front drop. Practise this until control is perfect. Always remember to take your legs back.

To do the half twist, as soon as your feet have left the bed and the body begins to fall face downwards, carry one arm strongly across the body, turning the head in the direction you wish to make the twist. You will then land in the back drop position.

To turn to the right, bring the left arm across and look to the right. The sketches show this being done.

To turn to the left, bring the right arm across and look to the left.

Keep your eyes on the bed for as long as possible during the twist.

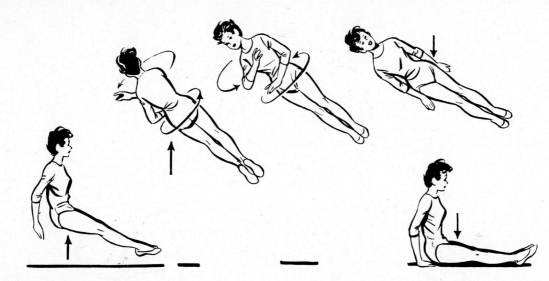

Seat Full Twist to Seat

The first essential is to perfect the seat drop. The next task is to make sure that the body is absolutely straight before initiating the twist. It is a good idea to practise this in two stages as follows:—

(a) Land on the seat in the normal seat drop position and then allow the hips to be lifted while the feet remain down on the bed. The body will then straighten. Practise this a number of times until the body is perfectly straight at an angle of about 30° to the bed.

(b) Next, as soon as the body is in this straightened position, throw the head in the required direction of the twist and bring the opposite arm or shoulder across.

The sequence of events is, seat bounce — extend — twist — seat bounce. Never try to twist until body has been straightened as this will carry you to the side of the trampoline.

Back Drop Forward Turn Over Half Twist to Back (The Cradle)

The problem is to combine the back drop learnt earlier with a front drop half twist to back drop, also learnt earlier. We suggest you practise as follows:—

(a) Practise front drop half twist to back, page 24.

(b) Practise a strong back drop giving plenty of forward momentum. Once you have this forward momentum and the bed coming towards you, carry arms strongly across body in the direction you wish to twist and make landing in the back drop position.

The cradle is the easiest to learn and looks best in competition with the twist being made after passing through the vertical position as shown above, but it can also be done with the twist being performed earlier i.e., before the vertical position is reached. Try both methods.

Somersault

Somersaulting has been purposely left until after the fundamentals because it is important to have mastered these properly before tackling any somersault movement.

Somersaulting means the complete rotation of the body forwards or backwards on the lateral axis.

Partial rotations are called "Turn Overs". These turn overs are used for build-up stages for the somersault proper.

The problem is to change up and down motion into forward or backward rotation. This is done by bending the body at the hips at the moment of take-off. It follows, therefore, that the secret of good somersaulting lies in correct hip action.

THE MECHANICS OF THE FRONT SOMERSAULT.

CORRECT FORWARD SOMERSAULT ACTION

Feet push forward and downward, hips move backward and upward and body rises and rotates vertically around the centre of gravity which remains directly above the take-off point. Landing is on the same point as the take-off.

keep head up

Do not throw head forward or downward as this reduces height and causes travel. Merely tuck chin in, if doing a "Turn Over", prior to back drop landing.

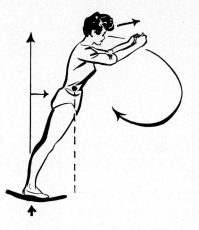

SOMERSAULT ACTION WITH FORWARD TRAVEL AND DIMINISHED HEIGHT IS INCORRECT.

When the centre of gravity is moved in front of the take-off point a forward somersault **with travel** will result because now the body is being pushed from behind as well as below, therefore it must travel forward up and over. Thus if you lean forward at take-off, you go forward.

NO SOMERSAULT ACTION

With centre of gravity directly over point of take-off, a somersault cannot occur provided there is no foot thrust backwards or forwards.

Front Somersault—*Initial Practice*

Remember, the first essential is to have control of all the fundamentals, otherwise success is unlikely.

The second is to be able to do a straight forward roll with the eyes open. This is to ensure that you can rotate forwards absolutely straight, and still be aware of your position when you come out of the roll. If you cannot do this you will never do a satisfactory somersault.

Once you have practised the forward roll and found that this can be done without losing sense of direction, there is no point in taking this action any further because the forward somersault differs from the forward roll in one very important respect. In the forward roll the head is thrown down between the legs and this sends the body down and over. In the forward somersault the hips must be lifted up over the head and this takes the legs up and over. In the forward roll the top half of the body is thrown down and under, while in the forward somersault the lower half of the body is lifted from the hips up and over.

1

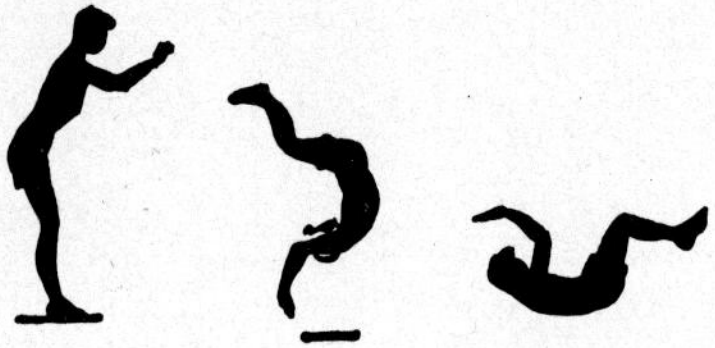

2

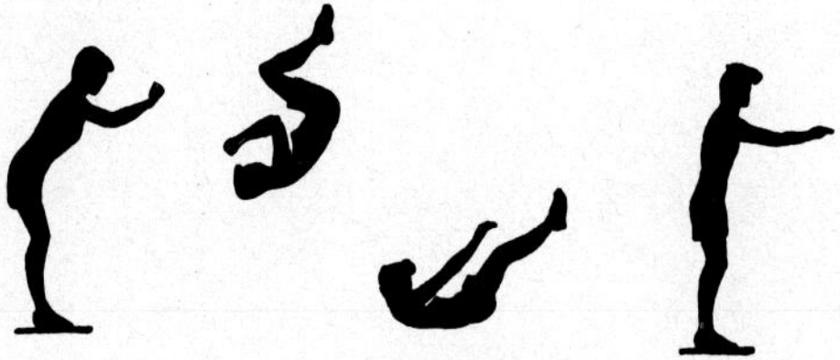

3

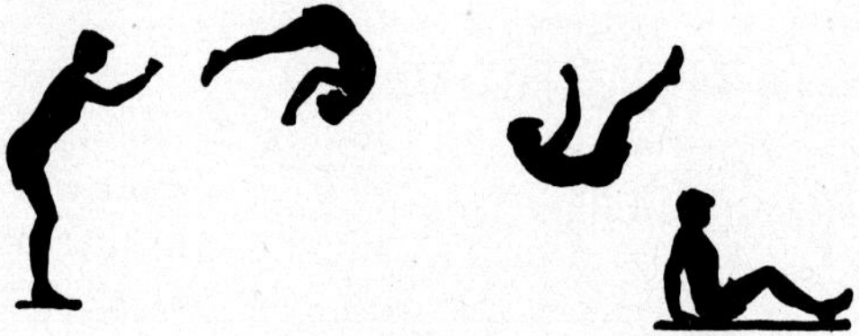

4

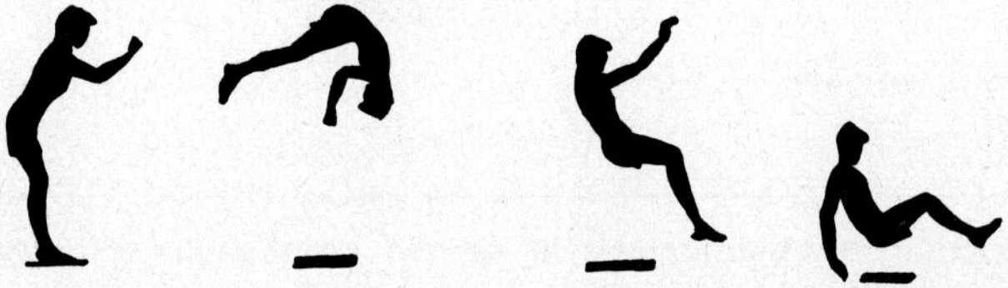

The progression then for forward somersault is as follows:—

1. The forward roll leaving the hands out ready to give support if necessary, but concentrating on lifting the hips a little more and landing on the back and rolling forward.

2. Same thing with a little bounce. More hip lift so that the trunk turns over, then bounce on to back and on to feet.

3. Same thing again with even more hip lift upwards and backwards landing in the seat drop. Keep knees apart so that nose is not bumped on knee.

4. Same thing again with even more hip lift, this time aiming at landing on the heels and falling backwards.

5. Same thing again with a really good vigorous take-off, hip lift very hard, landing this time on the feet with hands in front of the body as the landing is made (not illustrated).

Concentrate on the hip lift and avoid any forward travel by lifting the hips upwards and backwards. When practising this it is advisable to keep the arms in front in their normal position. It is advisable too, in the early stages, not to try and get into the tight tuck position because this would give too much spin and possible loss of control. It is better to learn the action slowly and then the tuck can be added later for effect and for faster rotation.

Forward Somersault

keep head up
at take-off

1. Take-off with strong hip drive upwards and slightly backwards. Don't throw head forward or down.

2. Continue driving the hips hard to lift them over the head.

3. Still think of keeping the hip drive going and this will place body in a loose tuck position.

4. Allow knees to bend to give a loose tuck position here and this helps to speed rotation.

5. An excellent tucked position is shown here but this is not really needed in the early stages of learning. Remember it is better in the early stages to under-spin rather than overspin.

6. Come out of the tuck in good time to avoid over-turning.

7. Lift the head before landing is made and extend body to check spin.

8. Land with arms forward to maintain balance and be ready for next movement.

Back Somersault

The back somersault cannot really be practised successfully without some form of assistance. It cannot safely be done in stages alone like the front somersault although it is possible to do one form of the back somersault (called the back pull-over) as a build-up stage from a back bounce. To do this, the performer drops on to his back, pulls on his knees and does a backward bounce-roll action on to his feet. This is not a satisfactory build-up stage for the back somersault as it makes the performer travel backwards which can be alarming and could be dangerous.

To learn the back somersault effectively some form of support is needed. The best support is to have the instructor holding you by a towel in the manner shown in the illustrations. A towel is preferred to a belt because a towel is thick and comfortable around the performer's body; it forms a thick and substantial grip for the instructor; it is absorbent and takes up the perspiration from the instructor's hand and there are no swivels, buckles or loops in which to catch his fingers. The towel is just wrapped around the performer once, twisted at the side, and gripped with one hand. This enables the instructor not only to support the performer throughout the entire movement but also to teach the essential movements as the exercise proceeds.

The illustrations show the correct grip for an instructor who is right-handed.

The essential movements for performing a back somersault are:—
1. A good strong arch of the body at take-off.
2. A tuck after the strong take-off has been made.
3. Good timing for a perfect landing position.

In the front somersault, forward rotation is obtained by throwing the hips backward and upward and in a similar fashion in the back somersault rotation is obtained by throwing the hips in the opposite direction i.e., forward and upward.

The sequence of practising is as follows:—

FIRST STAGE

1. The instructor stands behind the performer with his right hand on the nape of the performer's neck and his left hand holding the towel on the performer's left side.

2. They both begin to press down on the bed with a very low bounce, controlled so that they are both leaving and falling on the bed at exactly the same time. No attempt at somersaulting or any other movement should be made until this pair movement is co-ordinated.

3. The instructor then tells the performer to take off on the third bounce into a strong arch, backwards over the instructor's shoulder. The instructor explains that he will support the performer with one hand at the nape of the neck and the other hand at the waist.

4. The instructor's feet should be apart, one foot in front of the other as the take-off is made, see sketch.

5. The performer must have her head well back to ensure that the spine is arched from neck to hip. Throwing the head back also gives early vision of the bed and helps to stabilise the landing that will be made later on.

6. Instructor and pupil now proceed with this practice until the instructor is absolutely certain that the performer is getting a very strong arch take-off.

How does he know this? If the instructor is having to push very hard on the nape of the performer's neck to stop her going over, then obviously the performer's action must be correct.

SECOND STAGE

After the performer has got a strong arch, the second stage is to get her to repeat the take-off with a strong arch, but at the top of the bounce when she is above the instructor's head supported by the instructor's arms, then to pull her knees up to her chest. By changing from an extended position to a tight tuck position in the middle of the action it will be speeded up and the rotation will be completed without any trouble. Again the instructor holds her back from somersaulting until he is absolutely certain that she will make it. How will he know this? By the fact that if he has to work hard to stop her from going over and if he just got out of the way the performer would somersault without any trouble.

Note. The instructor's feet remain on the bed during this practice.

THIRD STAGE

For the last stage the instructor moves to the side of the performer, holding her by the towel at the side with one hand. If the instructor is right-handed he should stand on the performer's left side and hold the towel with his right hand. The performer now takes off on the third bounce as previously with a strong arch, followed by a tuck in the middle as practised and the instructor assists by pushing the back of the thighs if necessary to speed up the spin, and gripping the shoulder with the left hand to steady the performer as the landing is made.

Although performer and instructor are leaving the bed together on the first and second bounces, as the performer takes off, the instructor bends his knees to leave his feet flat and firm on the bed. The instructor gradually diminishes the amount of support given until the performer is accomplishing the somersault without any help at all.

Overhead Spotting Rig

The back somersault can also be taught using the overhead spotting rig shown on the right.

Before starting, check all ropes, knots, swivels, belts etc., for security.

Remember, the spotter grasps the rope at head height so that he can pull or release the rope and still have it under full control.

Performer must always jump below the exact centre of the rope and pulley to avoid pendulum swinging that could interfere with his correct action.

Be careful to take any kinks out of the rope so that it hangs straight in all directions.

The ropes attached to the belt should form an angle of about 45° with the side of the performer's body when standing still on the trampoline. This angle will prevent swivels on the belt from getting broken and give ample room for arm movements.

The 45° angle is a function of the height of the pulleys and their width. When the height of the pulleys is known then their proper distance apart to give correct angle can be calculated using this formula: —

Width apart of pulleys = twice height minus 13;
Measurements to the nearest foot in feet;
Example: Width = (20 ft. x 2) — 13 = 27 feet.

Back Somersault Feet to Feet

The first essential in a back somersault is to get a good strong arched take-off. The hips must be going forward and upward; the second sketch shows this strong arched position with the head well back.

The knees are then pulled up to the chest, the hands clasping the shins or close to the shins.

Later on the somersault can be performed without throwing the head backwards.

1. Remember not to lean back at take-off.

2. Lift the hips strongly upwards. A good arm lift gives additional height.

3. Head should still be well back looking for the bed. Bring the knees up to the chest to speed rotation.

4. Bed coming into view now. Hands ready to grasp shins is required for style but not really necessary to achieve just a single rotation.

5. This shows the ideal tight tuck position with eyes open. Tight tuck is good for competition and essential for double somersaults.

6. As soon as you catch sight of the bed, open the tuck to slow down the spin and avoid over turning.

7. Land with head slightly forward now and arms in front to prevent falling backwards.

8. Flex the knees and hips on landing to check the bounce or you will take off into another somersault.

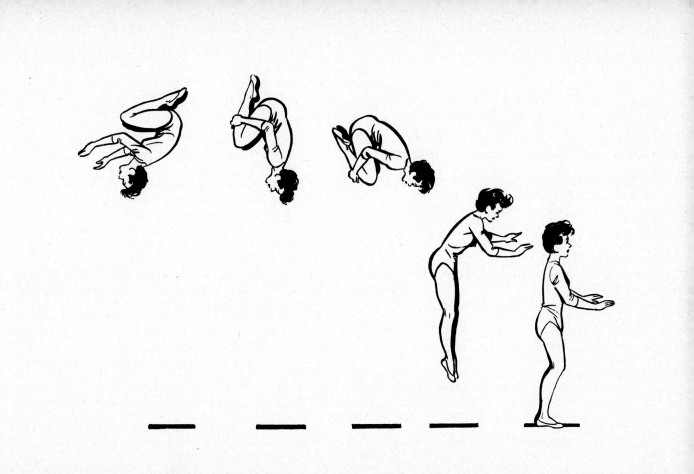

The Barany

The Barany is a form of forward somersault with a half twist, so the body lands facing in the opposite direction. It differs from the ordinary front somersault in this very important respect however, that the performer's eyes never lose sight of the bed. This makes it a very useful exercise as the performer should never lose control and can quickly change direction if need be.

It is similar in action to the round-off in ground work tumbling (see page 42).

There are a number of ways of teaching the Barany, some of them depending on manual assistance, but they will not be considered here as they are somewhat involved and require a very experienced instructor.

You can learn the Barany by yourself (but with spotters at the side rails of course) by following these stages:—

1. Knee bounce on the trampoline.
2. Knee bounce into a cartwheel along the trampoline making sure that both hands go on the red line of the trampoline as you put them down for the cartwheel action. The hips and legs come over the top of the arms and the landing is made with the knees astride the red line facing the opposite direction to the starting position.

It is very important that the eyes are fixed on the bed all the time.

The usual mistake is to take the arms out to the side of the trampoline instead of making sure that both hands are placed along the centre line of the bed. You can only get your hips and legs above your head if you put your hands directly in front of you. If you put your hands to your left then your body and legs will come round to the right and you will not get the correct somersault action.

3. Persist with stage 2 until gradually you can diminish the support you need on the hands.
4. Continue with stages 2 and 3 until the hands are no longer touching the bed and the Barany somersault, with eyes on the bed throughout, is being made from knees to knees.
5. Then try to get a stronger take-off from the knees so that the landing can be made, this time without the hands touching the bed, direct on to the feet.

Continue this until you are getting a really good lift and after that try feet to feet. Hands should be in front of the body all the time in the same way as for the cartwheel but not reaching downwards to touch the bed. Later, one hand can be taken up and the arm carried across the front of the body.

The secret of a good Barany, as it is a forward somersault movement, is in the strong hip action, i.e., the same as for the front somersault, hips going up and backwards. If difficulty is found in getting the twist action in this way, practise doing knee bounce to handstand, allowing the legs to fall past the vertical and then twisting as they fall to finish up in a knee bounce facing in the opposite direction.

An advantage of learning the Barany through the handstand position instead of a cartwheel position is that the hips are taken well up above the head before any twist is made. The twist in the Barany should occur at the peak of the bounce after a strong forward somersault movement has been initiated.

One disadvantage of learning the Barany through a cartwheel or handstand approach is that, like the forward roll build-up stage for the front somersault, it encourages turning the top half of the body downwards and this tends to reduce the lift from the bed. This disadvantage can be counteracted by a really strong hip lift at take-off.

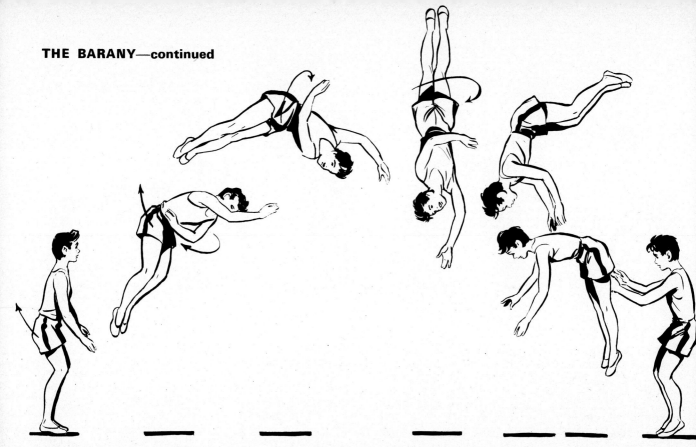

It is not necessary to extend one arm above the head but some people find this an easy transition from the cartwheel stage.

Dismounting from the Bed

Remember, for beginners the only real way to dismount is to walk to the end of the trampoline, place one hand on the rail and step down. Later, a number of other simple dismounts can be practised and these can be combined with known vaulting or agility exercises.

For example:

1. A simple dismount is to walk to the end of the bed, drop into a knee bounce, place the hands on the end rail and perform an overswing on to the feet, in the same way as you would do an overswing over a box horse. Make sure there is a landing mat.

2. The same exercise can be done with a half twist, similar to a Barany practice. This time a landing is made facing the bed. Practice can then be developed so that the hands no longer touch the end of the rail and the girl is doing a knee bounce Barany off on to the ground.

3. Another simple and attractive dismount is a back drop heave vault off. The performer walks to the end of the trampoline and places one foot on the end rail. The leading shin should be perpendicular and directly above the end rail and the hip should be forward, directly above the cables on the end. Then he lifts the rear leg forward and drops into a back drop right on the end of the bed with the seat on the cables. Not hurrying, he waits for the bed to lift him and shoot him forward, he pulls on the elastic cords, doing a heave vault over the end rail.

From the sketch a number of ways of learning this and assisting with this stunt can be seen. Remember to have a mat at the end of the trampoline. Do not attempt this stunt on a trampoline having steel spring suspension.

4. Another dismount is to adopt a kneeling position on the end of the trampoline, hands on the end rail, shoot the legs backwards and drop into a front drop with the chin held up 6 in. or so off the end rail. Gripping the bar, allow the legs to be lifted and then suddenly pull them through to perform a squat or through vault over the end of the rail with the knees passing between the hands. Make sure there are two spotters, one on each side, when learning this and the back drop heave vault dismount. Do not attempt this stunt on a trampoline having steel spring suspension.

Points to Remember

1. Remember that safety is of paramount importance. It involves being sure you have spotters all round, that you are not attempting stunts which are beyond your present ability, that you have clear overhead space to work, that you have not been jumping for too long and have become tired.

2. Remember that everything has to be learned and taught gradually, moving from what the performer already knows into a new movement.

3. Remember that the trampoline is a very powerful instrument and it does not discriminate between performers. If your movement is incorrect it will react the same way as it does to everybody else's incorrect movement and you could have an accident.

4. Remember with the somersaults, either forward or backward, the secret of success depends upon correct hip action. It is better only to accomplish a partial forward somersault without travel rather than to make a complete forward somersault, landing near the steel rail at the end. Take it gently, treat the trampoline with respect and be satisfied with a little progress.

5. Learning the backward somersault, make sure you are absolutely clear in your mind about what is required. A very strong arch take-off is needed to give rotation. You then need a tuck after the take-off has been made to speed up the rotation already given to the body. It is very important that these movements are done in exactly the order stated. A tuck when you have no rotation means trying to speed up something you haven't got. It is very important that you get the arch first and the tuck second.

6. In the Barany again aim at keeping the eye on the bed throughout. The Barany is a little unnatural to learn and therefore do not expect to make progress quite as rapidly with this stunt as you have with some of the others.

7. Remember that the hallmark of a good trampolinist is doing everything in or close to the centre of the trampoline.

8. Remember too that the aim is to combine exercises. Learn to do this by playing a little game called "Tag On" with your friends. It goes like this.

   The first performer jumps on and does a bounce. The second performer jumps on and has to do this bounce and add on another bounce of his own. The third performer jumps on and does the first bounce and the second bounce and has to add on a third bounce of his own. This goes on until there are so many bounces or the routine is so complicated that the last person is unable to do this, he is given some penalty or forfeit, he is also given the privilege of starting the next game off with his first bounce. This little game will quickly teach you what things form possible sequences.

9. When you are jumping on a trampoline it is very important that:

   1. A clear cut decision is made about exactly what is to be done.

   2. Next a clear cut decision is made about exactly when it is to be done i.e., on the third or the fourth bounce.

   3. By doing this you concentrate on the task at hand and also you prevent yourself from procrastinating the movement hoping that you are going to get a slightly better bounce if you continue jumping. It also enables the spotters to know exactly when you are going to make your move so that they can be ready to help you if required. For safety and success in all sports, concentration is most important.

Printed by Fretwell & Brian Ltd., Howden Hall, Silsden, Keighley, Yorks.